BENJAMIN WHITE

WRITING SKILLS HANDBOOK

Acquiring High-Performance Writing Techniques

Published in 2023 by Amba Press, Melbourne, Australia
www.ambapress.com.au

© Benjamin White 2023

All rights reserved. No part of this book may be reproduced or transmitted in any form or by any means, electronic or mechanical, including photocopying, recording or by any information storage and retrieval system, without prior permission in writing from the publisher.

Cover design: Tess McCabe
Editor: Rica Dearman

ISBN: 9781922607003 (pbk)
ISBN: 9781922607010 (ebk)

A catalogue record for this book is available from the National Library of Australia.

Contents

Introduction		1

The fundamentals of writing   2

Chapter 1	Understanding writing as a skill	3
Chapter 2	Basic grammar and punctuation	9
Chapter 3	Writing sentences and paragraphs	18

Developing your writing style   25

Chapter 4	Enhancing vocabulary	26
Chapter 5	Tone, voice, perspective	32

Types of writing   39

Chapter 6	Academic writing	40
Chapter 7	Creative writing	47
Chapter 8	Practical writing	54

Revising and editing   61

Chapter 9	Revising your work	62
Chapter 10	Avoiding common mistakes	67

Conclusion	The Writing Cycle	71
Final word	Specific tips for high school students	75

Introduction

Writing is one of the most important skills a person can have. It is essential for communication, getting a good job, expressing oneself creatively and solving problems. In today's world, where technology is reshaping the landscape of communication, the ability to express oneself articulately through written words is more important than ever.

This book, *Writing Skills Handbook*, is designed to help you develop your writing skills. It covers the basics of grammar and punctuation, sentence structure, paragraph construction, and style and tone. It also explores creative writing and practical writing, with chapters dedicated to exploring the unique challenges and opportunities that each form of writing presents.

The book concludes with a detailed discussion on revising and editing. Many students – like you, the reader – underestimate the importance of this stage, but it is through revising and editing that good writing truly becomes great. To that end, the book presents several strategies for self-editing, and discusses the valuable role that peer review and feedback can play in the writing process.

Writing Skills Handbook is divided into chapters, each of which focuses on a different aspect of writing. It includes exercises for you to complete that will help you learn and apply the concepts and skills discussed.

I hope this book helps you develop your writing skills. It won't happen overnight, but it will happen. Remember, writing is a journey, not a destination. It takes time and patience. But with practice (and this book helping you), you can become a great writer.

The fundamentals of writing

CHAPTER 1

Understanding writing as a skill

IN THIS CHAPTER

The significance of writing in high school and beyond

The role of writing

Writing – a skill for life

As a high school student, you stand at the cusp of adulthood. You might often find yourself questioning the relevance of various skills you are asked to learn. "Why do I need to learn algebra? When will I use it?" (Though, as an English and Literature teacher, I kinda get that one!) Among all the things you need to do at school, writing stands out as a particularly annoying one. Sitting down to write your essays is painful; where do you even start? In an era of digital communication and condensed textspeak and AI (Hi, ChatGPT!), you probably wonder why writing is so important. This chapter aims to answer that question.

The significance of writing in high school and beyond

Writing, particularly proficient writing, holds immense significance not only during your high school years, but it will also extend into your adult years. I, for example, am writing this book in my adult years, to help you survive writing in your high school years. In high school, writing is an essential tool for learning. Across various subjects, students are asked to write - essays in English or Literature, lab reports in Science, source analyses in History - writing is everywhere in your high school career. It helps to consolidate your learning, encourage the clear expression of thoughts and ideas, and develop your critical thinking skills.

Beyond high school, as you move into higher education or enter the workforce, writing takes on an even more important role. Universities and TAFE require written assignments, essays and dissertations. In the working world, the ability to write effectively can distinguish an individual in any job or field. This could be an email, a persuasive proposal, a detailed report or a motivational speech. The importance of writing will continue to grow throughout your life. That's why your teachers bang on about it, and that's why I've written this book.

The role of writing

Writing is more than just grammar or a collection of words on a piece of paper (or, most likely, a screen); it's a fundamental means of communication. When we write, we aren't merely creating sentences – we're conveying thoughts, sharing ideas and expressing emotions. It's a way for us to narrate stories, argue viewpoints and ask questions. Writing can persuade, inform, entertain and inspire. Whether we're writing a novel, drafting a business plan or texting a friend, the words we choose and how we arrange them impacts the effectiveness of our communication.

Writing also allows us to reach beyond the barriers of time and space. Words written today can resonate with readers many years in the future or across the globe. In this way, writing is a powerful tool for connection, capable of building bridges between cultures, generations and ideologies.

Writing – a skill for life

In a practical sense, effective writing aids in creating standout resumes and compelling cover letters, in articulating thoughts in professional and personal correspondence, and in expressing oneself on digital platforms. But the utility of writing extends beyond the practical. It offers a means of self-expression, a way to record memories, thoughts and dreams, and a medium to unleash creativity.

The process of writing also cultivates essential skills such as critical thinking, creativity and attention to detail. The need to structure thoughts logically, argue convincingly and select precise vocabulary enhances our cognitive abilities. Writing makes you smarter. As we grow and evolve, so does our writing.

In summary, writing is much more than an academic chore or a practical necessity – it's a vital life skill. Its importance in high school is undeniable, as it is embedded within all the classes you attend. However, its value extends far beyond, becoming a cornerstone of effective communication and a lifelong companion in both personal and professional spheres. The journey to master writing may seem daunting, but the rewards it reaps (good grades, a job, perhaps a girlfriend or boyfriend) are worth the effort. And I'm not just saying that because I'm an English teacher, or because I want you to buy this book (well, maybe I am, a little).

Activity: Communicate without words

Learning intention: To demonstrate the essential role writing plays in communication, and its power in expressing complex thoughts, ideas and emotions.

Instructions:

1. Pair up with a classmate.
    a. One of you will be the 'writer', the other the 'reader'.

2. The 'writer' should choose a simple scenario.
    a. For example, 'A girl receives a birthday present that she doesn't like but doesn't want to hurt the feelings of the person who gave it to her' (we've all been there).

3. Without using any words, the 'writer' should act out the scenario.
    a. This includes facial expressions, body language and sound effects. However, no actual words or signs can be used.

4. The 'reader' will then write down their interpretation of the scenario.
    a. What do they think is happening?
    b. How are the characters feeling?
    c. Why are they behaving this way?

5. Switch roles and repeat the activity.

6. Discussion
    a. How accurate were the 'reader's' interpretations?
    b. Did they fully capture the complexity of the scenario and the emotions of the characters? If not, why?

7. Reflection
    a. Reflect on this activity and write a paragraph about what you've learned about the power of words and written communication.

Extension: Written interview

Pair up with a classmate and conduct a 'written interview'. Each of you will prepare five open-ended questions, then provide written answers when you switch roles. Reflect on the process, discussing the strengths and challenges of written communication.

CHAPTER 2

Basic grammar and punctuation

IN THIS CHAPTER

Introduction to grammar
Sentence structure
Punctuation

Now, let's get into the building blocks of good writing: grammar and punctuation. Think of language as a building. Grammar provides the bricks and mortar – the components that give it structure. Punctuation is like the doors, windows and corridors – it guides the flow and pace of language, enhancing comprehension. Together, they form the basis of any written piece. Understanding them is fundamental to the development of robust writing skills.

Introduction to grammar

Grammar is the system that structures our language, and every language has its own set of grammatical rules. But grammar isn't about a set of ancient rules and memorising which word is what class. It's about understanding how words work together in a sentence to convey meaning. The building blocks of grammar include nouns, verbs, adjectives, adverbs, pronouns, prepositions, conjunctions and interjections.

Nouns	Nouns are words that represent people, places, things or ideas. They are often the *subjects* or **objects** in a sentence.
	For example, in the sentence, 'The *dog* chased the **ball**', both 'dog' and 'ball' are nouns. The dog is the *subject* of the sentence; the ball is the **object**.
Verbs	Verbs are action, or doing, words. They tell us what the subject of the sentence is doing.
	In the sentence, 'The dog **chased** the ball', 'chased' is the verb because it describes the action the dog is taking.

Adjectives	Adjectives describe of modify nouns. They provide more detail about a person, place, thing or idea. For example, in the sentence, 'The **small** dog chased the **red** ball', 'small' and 'red' are adjectives. They give us extra details about the dog (it's small) and extra information about the ball (it's red).
Adverbs	Adverbs modify verbs, adjectives or other adverbs. They often describe how, when, where and to what extent something is done. In the sentence, 'The dog chased the ball **quickly**', the word 'quickly' is the adverb because it tells us how the dog chased the ball.
Pronouns	Pronouns replace nouns to avoid repetition and make sentences flow better. Examples of pronouns include 'he', 'she', 'it', 'they' and 'we'. In the sentence, 'The dog chased the ball, **it** was very fast', 'it' is replacing 'the dog'.
Prepositions	Prepositions show the relationship between a noun (or pronoun) and another word in the sentence. They often indicate location, time, direction or manner. In the sentence, 'The dog chased the ball **in** the park', 'in' is a preposition telling us where the action took place.

Conjunctions	Conjunctions link words, phrases or clauses (more on them later) together. They include words like 'and', 'but', 'or' and 'so'. In the sentence, 'The dog chased the ball, **and** it caught it', 'and' is a conjunction that connects two clauses.
Interjections	Interjections are words or phrases that express strong emotions of reactions. They are often followed by an exclamation mark (!). Examples include 'oh', 'wow' and 'ouch'. An example of an interjection in this sentence is 'Oh!': '**Oh!** The dog caught the ball'. Everyone seems surprised the dog caught the ball.

Sentence structure

The English language has four basic types of sentence structure: simple, compound, complex and compound-complex. Effective and engaging writing uses a range of sentence structures to make sure the reader doesn't get bored. By varying the types of sentences you use in your writing, you create a more compelling narrative or argument. Let's look at a range of sentences, once again following the journey of our favourite dog.

Simple sentences

A simple sentence, also known as an independent clause (told you we'd come back to it), contains a subject and a verb and expresses a complete thought.

An example of a simple sentence is: 'The dog chased the ball.'

Compound sentences

Compound sentences contain two independent clauses joined together by a conjunction.

For example: 'The dog chased the ball, and it caught it, too.'

Here, 'the dog chased the ball' and 'it caught it, too' are independent clauses joined together by 'and'.

Complex sentences

Complex sentences contain an independent clause and at least one dependent clause.

A dependent clause is a group of words that don't make sense by themselves. We need more information for them to be coherent.

An example would be: 'Because the dog was fast, it caught the ball.'

Here, 'because the dog was fast' is the dependent clause (it doesn't make sense by itself), and 'it caught the ball' is the independent clause (it does make sense by itself.)

Complex sentences are generally introduced using subordinating conjunctions: because, if, since, when, etc.

Compound-complex sentences

Finally, the most intricate of the sentence structures: compound-complex.

A compound-complex sentence combines two independent clauses with at least one dependent clause.

An example is: 'The dog chased the ball, and it caught it, too, even though it was tired.'

'The dog chased the ball' and 'it caught it, too' are both independent clauses; 'even though it was tired' is the dependent clause.

Punctuation

Now we're getting down to the nitty-gritty. Punctuation, while seemingly minor, has a significant influence on a sentence's meaning. For instance, compare "Let's eat, grandma!" with "Let's eat grandma!" Here, a simple comma can be the difference between a friendly invitation and a rather gruesome proposition. Here's a crash course on the most common forms of punctation and where to use them:

- (.) **Full stops** are used to mark the end of a sentence.
- (,) **Commas** often act as a pause within a sentence, separating items in a list, clauses and various other elements.
- (;) **Semicolons** join closely related independent clauses.
- (:) **Colons** introduce a list, explanation or expansion on the previous clause.
- (") **Quotation marks**, as the name suggests, are used to quote speech or text verbatim, or to indicate titles of short works.

Each punctuation mark has specific rules for use that, when followed, contribute to the clarity of your writing. They guide the reader through your sentences, showing them where to pause, stop or expect an explanation.

Understanding basic grammar and punctuation rules is an important aspect of improving your writing skills. It enables you to convey your thoughts clearly and accurately, ensuring the reader interprets your message as intended. Armed with this knowledge, we can now progress to constructing well-composed sentences and structured paragraphs, which we will explore in the next chapter.

Activity: Sentence structure scavenger hunt

Learning intention: To reinforce your understanding of the four types of sentence structure and enhance the ability to identify them in various texts.

Instructions:

1. Find a variety of texts.
   a. These could include newspaper articles, short stories or even chapters from your favourite books. Aim for a range of different forms.

2. Identify the sentence structures.
   a. Go through the texts and highlight or underline sentences that you believe are examples of the different sentence structures. Mark simple sentences in one colour, compound sentences in another, complex in a third and compound-complex in a fourth.

3. Share your findings.
   a. After you've gone through your texts, gather with a group of classmates and share the sentences you've found. Discuss why you believe each sentence is a particular type. If there are disagreements, use them as a chance to build your knowledge of sentence structures.

4. Reflection.
   a. Write a short paragraph about this activity.
      i. Was it challenging to identify the different types of sentences?
      ii. Did the activity change the way you look at sentences and how they're constructed?
      iii. Did each different text type have a dominant type of sentence structure? Why do you think that is?

Extension: Building diverse sentences

Write a short story of your own. It should be about 200–300 words and include at least two examples of each sentence structure: simple, compound, complex and compound-complex. Share your story with a classmate and challenge them to identify the different types of sentences you've used.

CHAPTER 3

Writing sentences and paragraphs

IN THIS CHAPTER

Forming coherent sentences
Structuring paragraphs
Transitioning between paragraphs

With a firm understanding of the basics of grammar and punctuation, we can now dive into the art of writing by exploring the building blocks of any written piece: sentences and paragraphs. Here, we will cover forming coherent sentences, structuring paragraphs with a clear topic sentence, supporting sentences, and a concluding sentence, and effectively transitioning between paragraphs.

Forming coherent sentences

The sentence is the basic unit of language that expresses a complete thought. Forming coherent sentences requires not just grammatical accuracy, but also logical consistency and clarity of thought. Consider, for example, the sentence 'The fast, brown dog over the lazy fox jumped.' While it does contain all the necessary grammatical elements – noun, adjective, verb – the arrangement is confusing, making it hard to understand. A more coherent arrangement would be 'The fast, brown dog jumped over the lazy fox.'

Coherent sentences have clarity, precision and a logical sequence of thoughts. This comes from understanding the function of each word, ensuring subject-verb agreement, using correct verb tenses and arranging words in a way that accurately conveys the intended meaning. In short, coherence in a sentence is achieved by adhering to grammar rules and using them to guide the sentence's structure and content.

Functions of words	As we've discussed before, words serve different functions in sentences, based on their classes. Nouns typically act as subjects and objects, verbs convey actions or states of being, adjectives modify nouns, adverbs modify verbs, adjectives or other adverbs, and so on.
Subject-verb agreement	Subjects and verbs must agree in English. That is, if the subject is singular (the dog), the verb must also be singular (chases). If the subject is plural (the dogs), then the verb would be (chase).
Using correct verb tenses	Verb tenses indicate when an action takes place – in the past, present or future. Consistency in verb tense is important for clarity. If you start telling a story in the past tense, it's generally best to stick with that tense throughout the story. Shifting tenses without good reason is confusing for your audience.
Arranging words to convey meaning	The order of words in a sentence can dramatically impact its meaning. For example, 'The dog chased the cat' has a completely different meaning from 'The cat chased the dog'. Careful word placement helps you express exactly what you mean, avoiding potential confusion.

Structuring paragraphs

Once you master sentence construction, the next step is to group sentences into a larger unit of thought – a paragraph. A well-structured paragraph contains a topic sentence, supporting sentences and a concluding sentence.

The topic sentence presents the main idea of the paragraph. It sets the stage for what the paragraph will discuss and is usually the first sentence.

Supporting sentences follow the topic sentence, providing information, facts, examples or reasons that elaborate on the main idea. For instance, following the previous example, supporting sentences could discuss how reading improves vocabulary, enhances knowledge, stimulates creativity, and so on.

The concluding sentence summarises the main point or offers a closing thought related to the topic. It provides closure to the paragraph. Using the same example, a concluding sentence could be, 'With its multifaceted benefits, reading is a fundamental skill that fosters lifelong learning.'

Remember, each paragraph should focus on **one main idea**. If you find that a paragraph discusses multiple ideas, it may be best to break it into several paragraphs, each with its topic sentence and corresponding supporting sentences.

Transitioning between paragraphs

Transitioning effectively between paragraphs is essential to maintain the flow of the text and guide your reader through your line of thought. Transition words and phrases such as 'furthermore', 'on the other hand', 'for example', 'in conclusion' and many others provide this link, signalling the relationship between the ideas of two consecutive paragraphs.

For instance, if the second paragraph presents an opposing viewpoint to the idea discussed in the first, you might start with 'On the other hand' or 'However'. If you're adding more information to the same idea, 'Furthermore' or 'In addition' can be used. Sometimes, transition can also be achieved without specific transition words. You can use a concept or idea from the last sentence of the previous paragraph in the first sentence of the new one. This technique creates a 'bridge' between paragraphs, subtly guiding your reader from one idea to the next.

Mastering the art of forming coherent sentences and structuring paragraphs are foundational skills in writing. They allow you to communicate your ideas accurately and effectively, making your writing clear and compelling. As you continue to practise and apply these concepts, you'll find that your ability to express complex thoughts and arguments improves.

Activity: Paragraph puzzles

Learning intention: To understand the structure of paragraphs and how sentences within a paragraph relate and transition.

Instructions:

1. Select a paragraph.
    a. Choose a well-structured paragraph from a book, article or any reliable source. It should have a clear topic sentence, supporting sentences and a concluding sentence.
2. Deconstruct the paragraph.
    a. Write each sentence of the paragraph on a separate index card or piece of paper. Shuffle them.
3. Reconstruct the paragraph.
    a. Try to reconstruct the paragraph by arranging the sentences in their original order. Use your understanding of paragraph structure and flow of ideas to guide you.
4. Reflection.
    a. After you've reconstructed the paragraph, write a brief reflection. Some ideas for discussion could include:
        i. What clues helped you to identify the topic sentence, supporting sentences and concluding sentence?
        ii. Was it easy or challenging to figure out the order of sentences?
        iii. What did the activity teach you about how sentences within a paragraph relate?

Extension: Building your own paragraph puzzle

Using what you've learned by completing this activity, write a well-structured paragraph about a topic of your choice. Ensure it includes a clear topic sentence, supporting sentences and a concluding sentence. With a friend or classmate, repeat the activity on the previous page, but with your own paragraph, challenging your peer to organise your own writing.

Developing your writing style

CHAPTER 4
Enhancing vocabulary

IN THIS CHAPTER

The power of words: why vocabulary matters
Strategies to expand your vocabulary
Contextual understanding of words

Imagine trying to paint a vibrant landscape, but with only a handful of colours at your disposal. While you may still be able to create an image, the lack of variety would limit your capacity to fully capture the essence of the scene. The same applies to language. Words are the hues with which we paint the canvas of communication. The larger our vocabulary, the richer and more nuanced our expression becomes. This chapter explores the power of words, why vocabulary matters, strategies to expand your vocabulary and the importance of contextual understanding of words.

The power of words: why vocabulary matters

Vocabulary is the collection of words at a writer's disposal. It contributes to all aspects of language use, from speaking and reading to understanding and communicating effectively. But the role of vocabulary goes beyond mere utility; it is a powerful tool that allows us to express our thoughts, ideas and emotions with precision and finesse.

Vocabulary is the collection of words that we know and use. It's important for writing because it allows us to express our thoughts and ideas clearly and effectively. A strong vocabulary can help you to:

- Communicate complex thoughts and ideas.
- Differentiate between subtle shades of meaning.
- Convincingly argue a point of view.
- Command attention, respect and persuasion.
- Navigate the world with greater confidence.

On top of all that, having a strong grasp of vocabulary will help you, not only at school, but throughout your life. Remember, I did say that this book would help you when you leave the school gates. Have a look at how you can dominate social, creative, academic and professional settings with your solid grasp of the English language.

Social setting
- Make a good impression on others.
- Connect with people from different backgrounds.
- Express yourself clearly and creatively.
- Build stronger relationships.

Creative setting
- Write more engaging and impactful stories.
- Create more vivid and descriptive poems.
- Produce more persuasive arguments.
- Communicate your ideas more effectively.

Professional setting
- Communicate effectively with colleagues and clients.
- Make a good impression.
- Advance your career.
- Write clear reports and presentations.

Academic setting
- Understand different subjects.
- Contribute to the academic community.
- Understand complex essays and articles.
- Perform better on exams.

Strategies to expand your vocabulary

Now, I know this book is about writing. But reading and writing are closely linked. You can't really have one without the other. Take this book, for example: if you couldn't read, then you wouldn't be able to use this to improve your writing. So, with that said, here are some effective strategies:

♦ **Read extensively:**
- Reading is the most effective way to enhance vocabulary. Dive into diverse genres of books, newspapers, journals or online articles. Encountering words in various contexts will aid in remembering them and understanding their usage.

- **Use a dictionary and thesaurus:**
  - Make it a habit to look up unfamiliar words in a dictionary. A thesaurus can introduce you to synonyms and antonyms, adding more dimensions to your word knowledge.
- **Learn a word-of-the-day:**
  - Many 'word-a-day' calendars or apps are available that introduce you to a new word daily. Make it a point to learn it and use it in your conversations or writing. You can even get word-of-the-day toilet paper!
- **Play word games:**
  - Games like Scrabble, Boggle or crossword puzzles are not only fun, but are also excellent tools for vocabulary expansion. The COVID-19 pandemic also brought to life Wordle, another great way to practise and develop your vocabulary.
- **Practise writing:**
  - Here's one out of left field. Regular writing, be it journaling, essay writing or creative writing, forces you to recall and use words, reinforcing your vocabulary in the process.
- **Learn roots, prefixes and suffixes:**
  - Many English words are based on Latin and Greek roots. Knowing these can help you deduce the meaning of unfamiliar words. I've written another book – *Reading Skills Handbook* – which has some suggestions around this.
- **Use online resources:**
  - There are many great online resources for learning new words. Some good ones you may want to bookmark for your next assessment task are:
    - Vocabulary.com – **www.vocabulary.com**
    - Macquarie Dictionary – **www.macquariedictionary.com.au**
    - Dictionary.com – **www.dictionary.com**
    - Thesaurus.com – **www.thesaurus.com**
    - Khan Academy – **www.khanacademy.org**

Contextual understanding of words

Expanding your vocabulary isn't just about memorising words; it's about understanding them in context. Contextual understanding refers to how the meaning of a word can change based on the words that surround it. Consider the word 'run', for example. Its meaning changes drastically in different contexts: 'run a business', 'run in the park', 'run an idea', 'run a fever'.

When learning a new word, it's important to pay attention to how it's used in context. This will help you understand the word's meaning and to use it correctly in your own writing. Pay attention to how words are used in sentences, the prepositions they're paired with or the context they're commonly used in.

Activity: Word collector

Learning intention: To enhance vocabulary and understand the contextual usage of new words.

Instructions:

1. Start a word journal.
   a. Each day for a week, select five unfamiliar words from your reading, or your talking, or your viewing, or your scrolling. Write these words in your word journal.
2. Define and use.
   a. For each word, write down its definition from a dictionary. Then, write a sentence using the word in the context you found it. This will help you understand how the word is used in sentences.
3. Share and discuss.
   a. At the end of the week, share some of your words with classmates. Discuss their meanings and the sentences you wrote. This can lead to interesting conversations and more learning.
4. Reflection.
   a. Reflect on how this activity has helped expand your vocabulary. Some suggestions to prompt your thinking:
      i. Did you find yourself recognising these words in other contexts?
      ii. How have these new words enriched your understanding of expression?

Extension: Word application stories

Write a short story using at least 10 of the new words you've collected in your journal. Try to use the words in a way that clearly shows their meaning. Share your story with a classmate and see if they can identify the words you've used and understand their meaning from the context.

CHAPTER 5

Tone, voice, perspective

IN THIS CHAPTER

Defining and distinguishing tone, voice and perspective

How to develop your unique writing voice

Writing from different perspectives

Writing is not merely about correctly stringing words together; it's also about the subtleties that give life to those words. Three such subtleties are tone, voice and perspective. They shape the reader's perception and interpretation of your writing. This chapter aims to define and distinguish tone, voice and perspective, and guide you on developing your unique writing voice and writing from different perspectives.

Defining and distinguishing tone, voice and perspective

Tone, voice and perspective are three important elements of writing. They all contribute to the overall meaning and impact of a piece of writing.

- **Tone** refers to the attitude or emotion that your writing conveys. It's influenced by the choice of words (diction), their arrangement (syntax) and the use of stylistic devices like metaphors or similes. For example, a tone could be formal, informal, playful, serious, sarcastic or sombre, depending on the context and audience.
- **Voice** is the distinct personality or style of the writer that's reflected in their writing. It's what makes each writer unique, like a vocal fingerprint. Your voice might be humorous, passionate, objective, subjective, analytical or descriptive. It is influenced by your unique experiences, values and perceptions.
- **Perspective** refers to the point of view from which the story is told. It's the lens through which the writer views and presents the narrative. The first-person perspective uses 'I', the second person uses 'you', and the third person uses 'he', 'she', 'it' or 'they'.

While these three elements are distinct, they're interconnected. The writer's voice is often consistent across their works, giving them their unique style. Tone, on the other hand, can vary based on the subject or audience. Perspective can shape both the voice and the tone by determining who is telling the story and how they are telling it.

For example, a writer might use a formal tone in a research paper to convey their authority on the subject. However, they might use a more informal tone in a blog post to connect with their audience on a personal level. The writer's voice might also change depending on the subject. For example, a writer might use a humorous voice in a story about a funny experience, but a more serious voice in a story about a difficult experience.

How to develop your unique writing voice

Developing your writing voice is a gradual process that involves self-exploration and practice. It's important for all writers, regardless of their experience and skill level. Here are a few tips to help you develop your one-of-a-kind, unique, totally fresh writing voice:

- **Read widely.** Here I go again! Reading exposes you to different writing styles, broadening your understanding of voice in writing. Pay attention to the tone, voice and perspective of the authors you read. What do you like about their writing? What could they improve on?

- **Write regularly.** The reason we're all here. The more you write, the more you'll understand your natural style. Over time, you'll be able to refine and define your voice. Try writing in different genres, such as fiction, non-fiction, poetry and essays. Experiment with different tones and voices.

- **Reflect your personality.** Allow your personality, beliefs and values to shine through your writing. Your voice is essentially an extension of who you are. There's only one of you on this planet, after all. What are you passionate about? What are your unique experiences? What makes you laugh, cry, get angry?

- **Experiment with styles.** Try out different writing styles and tones until you find what feels most comfortable and genuine to you. Don't be afraid to experiment with different techniques, such as imagery, metaphor and symbolism.

- **Seek feedback.** Having others read your work can give you valuable insights into your writing voice – and I'm not just talking about your teacher here. Whoever you give your writing to may notice consistent patterns or themes that you might overlook. Ask for feedback from friends, family or writing mentors.

Developing your writing voice takes time and effort, but it's an important part of the writing process. Over time, it will help you to become a better writer. By following these tips, you can start to develop your own unique voice that will connect with your readers on a personal level.

Writing from different perspectives

Choosing a perspective is crucial as it determines how the reader experiences your narrative. There are three main perspectives that writers can use: first person, second person and third person.

- **First-person perspective** gives a personal and intimate account of events, as the narrator is a character in the story. This perspective is often used in fiction, but it can also be used in non-fiction, such as memoirs or personal essays. First-person perspective can be a powerful tool for conveying personal experiences and emotions. It allows the reader to connect with the narrator on a deeper level.

- **Second-person perspective** addresses the reader directly, making them a part of the narrative. This perspective can make your writing more engaging and immersive. Second-person perspective can be used to create a sense of immediacy and involvement in the story. It can also be used to challenge the reader's perspective or to make them think about things in a new way.

- **Third-person perspective** offers a more detached view, as the narrator isn't a character in the story. This perspective is often used for academic writing, reporting or when you want to present an objective analysis. Third-person perspective can be used to create a sense of objectivity and neutrality. It can also be used to explore multiple perspectives on a single event.

The best perspective for your writing will depend on the genre, your purpose and your audience. If you're writing a memoir or personal essay, first-person perspective may be the best choice. If you're writing a report or academic paper, third-person perspective may be more appropriate. And if you're writing a story that you want to be both engaging and immersive, second-person perspective may be the way to go.

Activity: Tone and voice detectives

Learning intention: To enhance understanding of tone, voice and perspective in writing.

Instructions:

1. Choose a short story or novel that you think would be appropriate for your level.
2. Read the story carefully and pay attention to the tone, voice and perspective.
3. Use the following questions to guide your thinking:
    a. What is the tone of the story? Is it serious, humorous, suspenseful, etc.?
    b. What is the voice of the story? Is it formal, informal, objective, subjective, etc.?
    c. What is the perspective of the story? Is it told from the first-person, second-person or third-person point of view?
4. Once you have a good understanding of the tone, voice and perspective of the story, write a summary of the story, including your thoughts on how the author uses these elements to create a particular effect on the reader.
5. If you are feeling ambitious, you can write your own short story or novel, using different tones, voices and perspectives.

Extension: Creating voices

Now that you have a handle on tone, voice and perspective, try this extension activity. Select a simple event, like a day at school or a family dinner. Write a short story of this event three times, each time using a different tone, voice and perspective.

Types of writing

CHAPTER 6

Academic writing

IN THIS CHAPTER

Essays: narrative, descriptive, expository and persuasive

Research papers: a step-by-step guide

Citations and avoiding plagiarism

Academic writing is a key skill for high school students, serving as a cornerstone for assignments, exams and university application essays. It refers to a style of expression that researchers and students use to define the intellectual boundaries of their disciplines and their areas of expertise. This chapter delves into the types of essays you may encounter, the process of writing research papers, and the importance of citations and avoiding plagiarism.

Essays: narrative, descriptive, expository and persuasive

Let's be honest, the reason you're here is because you probably have an essay due for a subject and you need to smash it out the night before. I may be a teacher, but I know how students operate. Mainly because I did the exact same thing in high school. So, the essay, let's get to it. In high school, you'll likely be asked to write four types of essay: narrative, descriptive, expository and persuasive. Each type of essay has its own unique purpose and structure.

- **Narrative essays** tell a story about a personal experience. They require a clear point of view, sensory details and an orderly sequence of events. For example, you could write a narrative essay about your first day of high school, your summer vacation or a challenging experience you've overcome.

- **Descriptive essays** require you to describe something – a person, place, object or event – in such a way that the reader can clearly visualise it. They often employ vivid language and detail. For example, you could write a descriptive essay about your favourite animal, your dream vacation destination or a painting you saw in a museum.

- **Expository essays** explain a topic. They are based on facts, not personal feelings, requiring you to provide evidence and examples to support your points. For example, you could write an expository essay about the history of World War II, the benefits of exercise or the dangers of smoking.

- **Persuasive essays** present a claim and evidence to support that claim. They require you to research, generate and evaluate evidence, and to establish a position on a topic. For example, you could write a persuasive essay about whether homework should be banned, whether or not animals should be used in research or whether or not essays are a good thing to do at school.

No matter what type of essay you're writing, it's important to remember that all essays have a common structure: an introduction, body paragraphs and a conclusion. The introduction should grab the audience's attention and introduce the topic of the essay. The body paragraphs should support the main contention with evidence and examples. The conclusion should summarise the main points of the essay and restate the thesis statement.

Research papers: a step-by-step guide

You may not have to complete a research paper at high school, but you will have to complete one at university – if you decide to go to university that is, and not take a gap year galivanting around Europe with your mates... Anyway, research papers. Here's a crash course on how to get started on one:

1. **Choose a topic.** The first step is to choose a topic that you're interested in (or whatever topic you've been assigned in your course) and one that you can find enough information about.

2. **Develop a thesis statement.** The thesis statement is the main point of your paper. It should be clear, concise and arguable.

3. **Do your research.** This is where you'll gather all your information on your topic. You can find information in books, academic journals, reputable websites and primary sources.

4. **Draft your paper.** Once you have your research, you can start drafting your paper. Be sure to follow the outline you created in step 2.

5. **Revise your paper.** After you have a draft of your paper, take some time to revise it. Check for errors in grammar and spelling, and make sure your argument is logically structured and supported.

Citations and avoiding plagiarism

In academic writing, it is important to cite your sources and avoid plagiarism. This is because citations give credit to the original author of the work and allow readers to find the source for themselves. Plagiarism, on the other hand, is a form of academic dishonesty that can have serious consequences. There are a few different ways to cite sources in academic writing. The most common styles are MLA and APA. It is important to use the style that your instructor prefers.

♦ To cite a source in **MLA style**, you would include the author's last name, the title of the work, the publication information and the page number(s) of the material you are citing. For example, if you are citing a book by William Shakespeare called *Romeo and Juliet,* you would write the following citation:

- Shakespeare, William. *Romeo and Juliet.* Edited by G Blakemore Evans, Arden Shakespeare, 1984.

♦ To cite a source in **APA style**, you would include the author's last name, the year of publication, the title of the work, the publication information and the page number(s) of the material you are citing. For example, if you are citing the same book by William Shakespeare in APA style, you would write the following citation:

- Shakespeare, W (1984). *Romeo and Juliet.* Edited by G Blakemore Evans. Arden Shakespeare.

It is also important to avoid plagiarism when paraphrasing or quoting sources. When you paraphrase, you put the author's ideas into your own words. When you quote, you use the author's exact words. In both cases, you need to cite the source.

- To paraphrase a source, you should read the original text carefully and then write your own version of it. You should not simply change a few words or phrases from the original text. You should also cite the source of your paraphrase.
- To quote a source, you should copy and paste the author's exact words. You should also cite the source of your quote, including the page number(s) where the quote appears.

Activity: Mini research paper

Learning intention: To learn the essential skills of academic writing, including choosing a topic, gathering information, writing a thesis statement, organising a paper, revising and editing, and citing sources.

Instructions:

1. Choose a topic for your research paper that is both interesting and appropriate for the assignment.
2. Gather information from reliable sources and take good notes.
3. Write a clear and concise thesis statement.
4. Organise your paper logically and support your thesis statement with evidence from your research.
5. Revise and edit your paper for grammar, spelling and clarity.
6. Cite your sources correctly to avoid plagiarism.

Extension: Peer review session

Organise a peer review session with your classmates. Each student should come with a draft of their mini research paper. During the session, take turns giving feedback on each other's work, focusing on the argument, the support provided by the research, and the overall structure and flow of the paper.

CHAPTER 7

Creative writing

IN THIS CHAPTER

Elements of a story
Writing prompts to spark creativity
Revising and editing your work

While academic writing is structured and formal, creative writing lets your imagination soar. It involves crafting stories filled with compelling characters, vibrant settings and engaging plots. This chapter delves into the elements of a story, offers writing prompts to spark creativity and provides tips for revising and editing your work.

Elements of a story

The elements of a story are the building blocks that make up a good narrative. By understanding these elements, you can write better stories, analyse stories more effectively and appreciate stories more fully.

Plot	The plot is the sequence of events in your story. It typically includes an introduction, rising action, climax, falling action and resolution. The introduction introduces the setting, characters and conflict. The rising action builds up the tension and suspense. The climax is the most exciting point in the story, where the conflict is resolved. The falling action brings the story to a close. The resolution ties up any loose ends.
Setting	The setting refers to the time and place where your story unfolds. It creates a backdrop against which the characters act and the plot unfolds. A vividly described setting can help readers visualise the story.

Character	Characters are the individuals who inhabit your story. They can be people, animals or even inanimate objects, depending on the narrative. Developing believable characters with distinct personalities and motivations makes your story more engaging.
Conflict	Conflict is the challenge or problem that the characters face. It drives the plot and influences character development. Conflict can be internal (within a character's mind) or external (between characters or between a character and their surroundings).
Theme	An English teacher's favourite thing to carry on about. The theme is the underlying message or big idea of your story. It's the thread that ties the elements of your story together. Themes can be complex ideas like love, justice or identity, or simple lessons or morals.
Perspective	The point of view determines who is telling the story and what information they can provide. This could be first person ('I'), second person ('you') or third person ('he', 'she', 'it' or 'they'). If you want more info on perspective, just go back a few pages.

Writing prompts to spark creativity

Writing prompts can help you overcome writer's block, explore different ideas and improve your writing skills. Here are a few prompts to inspire you:

- **Start with a line:** 'I had never seen anything like it before.' What is it that you have never seen before? Where are you when you see it? What happens next?

- **Open a door:** Imagine you found a door in your house that you had never noticed before. What happens when you open it? Is it a portal to another world? A secret passage? Or something else entirely?

- **Write from a different perspective:** Write a story from the perspective of a stray dog wandering the streets. How does the world look from their point of view? What challenges do they face? What dreams do they have?

- **Discover a superpower:** Create a tale where the main character discovers they have a superpower. What kind of superpower is it? How does it change their life? What challenges do they face with their newfound power?

- **Write in a different world:** Write a story set in a world where everyone can read minds. How does this change society? How does it affect relationships? What are the challenges of living in a world where everyone knows what you're thinking?

- **Online resources:** There are heaps of online resources you can access to help you overcome writer's block and get the creative juices flowing. Here are some kick you off:

    - The Writing Cooperative: www.writingcooperative.com
    - Writer's Digest: www.writersdigest.com/be-inspired/writers-digest-best-creativity-websites-2023
    - StoryADay: www.storyaday.org
    - Reddit: www.reddit.com

- Reddit has a number of subreddits dedicated to creative writing. These are a great place to find writing prompts, feedback on your work and a community of writers to connect with.

Revising and editing your work

Creative writing is a journey of exploration and imagination. It allows you to express your thoughts, feelings and ideas in unique and innovative ways. However, even the best writers need to revise and edit their work to make it the best it can be.

Revising and editing is the process of making changes to your writing to improve its clarity, coherence, grammar and spelling. It can also involve making changes to the plot, characters, setting or theme of your story.

Here are some tips for revising and editing your work:

- **Give it time:** After you finish writing, take a break before you start revising. This allows you to approach your work with fresh eyes and a clear mind.
- **Read aloud:** Reading your work aloud helps identify awkward sentences, word repetitions and areas where the flow might be off.
- **Check for clarity:** Make sure your plot is logical, your characters are believable and your setting is vividly described.
- **Proofread:** Look for typos, grammatical errors, punctuation mistakes and incorrect word usage.
- **Seek feedback:** Share your work with others and be open to their feedback. Different perspectives can help identify strengths and weaknesses in your work.

Remember, revising and editing is an important part of the creative writing process. By taking the time to revise and edit your work, you can make it the best it can be.

Activity: Story time!

Learning intention: To understand elements of a story and apply them in creative writing.

Instructions:

1. **Story elements review:** Review the elements of a story: plot, setting, characters, conflict, theme and perspective. Understand how these elements interplay to form a compelling narrative.
   a. Plot is the sequence of events in a story. It typically includes an introduction, rising action, climax, falling action and resolution.
   b. Setting is the time and place where a story unfolds. It creates a backdrop against which the characters act and the plot unfolds.
   c. Characters are the individuals who inhabit a story. They can be people, animals or even inanimate objects, depending on the narrative.
   d. Conflict is the challenge or problem that the characters face. It drives the plot and influences character development.
   e. Theme is the underlying message or big idea of a story. It's the thread that ties the elements of a story together. Themes can be complex ideas like love, justice or identity, or simple lessons or morals.
   f. Perspective determines who is telling the story and what information they can provide. This could be first person ('I'), second person ('you') or third person ('he', 'she', 'it' or 'they').

2. **Brainstorm:** Choose a prompt from the list provided or come up with your own. It could be as simple as 'A day at the zoo' or as intriguing as 'The mystery of the abandoned house'. Use this prompt to brainstorm ideas for your plot, setting, characters, conflict, theme and point of view.

3. **Write your story:** Using your brainstormed ideas, write a short story. Make sure your story incorporates all the elements and creates an engaging narrative.

4. **Revise and edit:** Review your story, paying attention to the narrative flow, character development, conflict resolution and overall coherence. Revise and edit your work for clarity, grammar and punctuation.

5. **Share and discuss:** Share your story with a classmate. Provide each other with constructive feedback, focusing on how well each story element was developed and incorporated into the narrative.

Extension: 'Story exchange'

Swap stories with a classmate and rewrite their story from a different character's point of view or change the setting, conflict or theme. This exercise challenges you to approach a narrative from a new perspective and adapt your writing accordingly.

CHAPTER 8

Practical writing

IN THIS CHAPTER

Writing emails and letters
Writing resumes and cover letters
Writing for social media

I've called this chapter 'Practical writing', but I'm not sure why, because all writing is inherently practical. You want to entertain, inform or persuade. These are all practical applications of writing. Anyway, this chapter focuses on the types of writing you might do at work or in the world outside the classroom – the 'real world'. From emails and letters to resumes and cover letters and social media posts, every form of writing requires a unique style and approach.

Writing emails and letters

Emails and letters are essential forms of communication, both in school and in the workplace. A well-written email or letter can convey your message clearly and effectively, and it can make a good impression on the recipient.

Here are some tips for writing effective emails and letters:

- **Start with a clear subject line.** The subject line should give the recipient a brief overview of what your email or letter is about.

- **Use a courteous salutation.** If you are writing to someone you don't know well, use 'Dear Mr/Ms [Last Name]' or 'To Whom It May Concern'. If you are writing to someone you know, you can use their first name.

- **Be clear and concise.** Get to the point quickly and avoid rambling.

- **Use proper grammar and spelling.** Proofread your email or letter carefully before sending it.

- **End with a polite sign-off.** If you are writing to someone you don't know well, use 'Sincerely', 'Best regards' or 'Thank you for your time'. If you are writing to someone you know, you can use something less formal. 'Many thanks', 'Thanks' or 'Cheers' are good choices.

Here are some examples of different types of emails and letters:

- **Formal email:** A formal email is typically used for business or academic purposes. It should be brief, clear and respectful.
- **Personal email:** A personal email is typically used to communicate with friends and family. It can be more informal and expressive.
- **Cover letter:** A cover letter is a document that you send with your resume when you are applying for a job. It should introduce yourself and explain why you are interested in the position.
- **Thank you letter:** A thank you letter is a way to express your gratitude for something that someone has done for you. It can be sent after a job interview, a meeting or receiving a gift.

Writing resumes and cover letters

Resumes and cover letters are essential tools for jobseekers. They are a way to showcase your skills, experience and qualifications to potential employers. A well-written resume and cover letter can help you get your foot in the door and land the job you want.

Here are some tips for writing effective resumes and cover letters:

- **Start with a strong objective statement.** This is a brief statement that summarises your career goals and why you are interested in the job you are applying for.
- **List your education and work experiences in reverse chronological order.** Start with your most recent education and work experience and work your way back.
- **Highlight your key skills and achievements.** What are the skills and experiences that make you a valuable candidate for the job? Be sure to highlight these in your resume and cover letter.
- **Use keywords throughout your resume and cover letter.** When you are applying for a job, be sure to use keywords that are relevant to the job description. This will help your resume and cover letter get noticed by potential employers.
- **Proofread your resume and cover letter carefully before submitting them.** Typos and grammatical errors will make you look unprofessional. Take the time to proofread your documents carefully before you hit send.

Here are some additional tips for writing resumes and cover letters:

- **Tailor your resume and cover letter to the specific job you are applying for.** Don't just send out the same resume and cover letter to every job you apply for. Take the time to read the job description carefully and tailor your documents to the specific requirements of the job.

- **Get feedback from others.** Ask a friend, family member or teacher to review your resume and cover letter and give you feedback. This can help you identify any areas that need improvement.

- **Use online resources.** There are many online resources available that can help you write effective resumes and cover letters. Be sure to do your research and find resources that are credible and up to date.

Writing for social media

I've no doubt that the person reading this is a budding social media influencer. You have 1,000 friends on Facebook (if that's still a thing), 1 million followers on Instagram and have made a viral TikTok. Nevertheless, it's still important to be able to communicate clearly on social media using the written word. We all know that social media is a powerful tool for communication and engagement. It can be used to connect with friends and family, share information and build a brand. But to be effective, it's important to know how to write for social media.

Here are some tips for writing effectively for social media:

- **Know your audience.** Who are you writing for? What are their interests? What kind of language do they use? Tailor your writing to your target audience.

- **Be concise.** People have short attention spans on social media. Get to the point quickly and use clear, concise language.

- **Use visuals.** Images and videos can help to break up your text and make your posts more visually appealing.

- **Engage with your audience.** Ask questions, solicit feedback and encourage comments. This will help to keep your audience engaged and coming back for more.

- **Proofread.** Even on social media, it's important to proofread your posts for errors in grammar and spelling.

Activity: Writing professionally and socially

Learning intention: To be able to write a well-structured and engaging email to a potential employer.

Instructions:

1. Scenario:
    a. You've just finished Year 10 and you're ready for the summer holidays. Unfortunately, you need to finance your big summer plans. You're going to have to apply for a job. You've seen a position for a Social Media Marketing Assistant in the local paper. Write an email to the company's creative director introducing yourself and why you'd be perfect for the job.

Extension: Showing what you can do

Good news! You've managed to score an interview for the position of Social Media Marketing Assistant. They want to meet you and suss you out, but on top of that, they want to see what you can do for their social media accounts. Construct a social media post for the company (you can choose which company and what they do) advertising some of their products and/or introducing yourself as the new Marketing Assistant.

Revising and editing

CHAPTER 9
Revising your work

IN THIS CHAPTER

Why revision matters
Self-editing techniques
Peer review and feedback

Well look at that, you've made it to the end of the book! Now comes the fun part. Years of teaching English and essay writing has led me to this conclusion: students don't enjoy editing and revising their work before submitting it. You just focus on getting it done on time. Well, I hate to tell you this, but the essence of writing is rewriting. Revision is the process that takes your work from a rough collection of ideas to a polished piece of communication.

Why revision matters

Revision is a critical step in the writing process, often determining the difference between good writing and great writing. It is during this phase that you can refine your ideas, clarify your arguments, improve your sentences and correct grammar and spelling mistakes. In essence, revision is the process through which you ensure your writing effectively communicates your intended message in the most engaging and clear manner possible.

Self-editing techniques

Revising your own work can be a challenging process, requiring a critical eye and attention to detail. Here are some strategies to help:

- **Take a break:** After you finish writing, take some time away from your work. This break can give you fresh perspective when you return to revise.

- **Read aloud:** Reading your work aloud can help you notice awkward sentences, repetition or inconsistencies that you might overlook when reading silently.

- **Look for common errors:** Keep a list of common errors you tend to make, and search for them during your revisions.

- **Check for clarity:** Make sure each sentence, paragraph and section is clear and contributes to your overall argument or story. Remove or revise any parts that seem confusing or unnecessary.

- **Revise in stages:** Trying to revise everything at once can be overwhelming. Consider revising in stages – first looking at the overall structure and organisation, then sentence clarity and word choice, and finally grammar and punctuation.

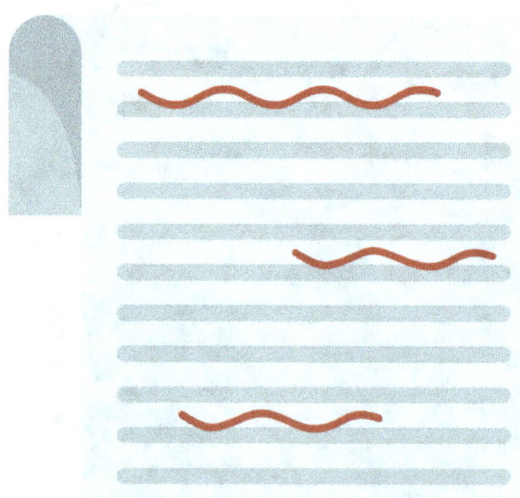

Peer review and feedback

While self-editing is important, getting feedback from others is equally valuable. Other people can provide a fresh perspective and catch mistakes or confusing parts that you might have missed. Here are some tips for effective peer review:

- **Find a trusted reviewer:** Choose someone who is knowledgeable about the topic or skilled in writing. Their feedback will be more valuable and accurate.
- **Be open to criticism:** It's natural to feel defensive about your work but try to keep an open mind. Remember, the goal is to improve your writing, and constructive criticism is a tool to help you achieve this.
- **Ask specific questions:** To get the most useful feedback, ask your reviewer specific questions. Instead of just asking if your work is 'good', ask if your argument is clear, if your evidence is convincing or if your characters are believable.
- **Consider all feedback:** Review all the feedback you receive, but remember, you don't have to make every suggested change. Consider the feedback, but ultimately, decide what works best for your piece.
- **Revise based on feedback:** Use the feedback to make revisions. This might involve reworking sections, clarifying points, fixing errors or even rewriting the piece entirely.

Revision is an ongoing process of refinement, a dance of adding, deleting and reworking until your piece communicates your message in the best possible way. It can be challenging and time-consuming, but it is a necessary step to ensure your writing is clear, polished and impactful.

Activity: The revision dance

Learning intention: You will be able to revise your writing using a variety of strategies to improve clarity, flow and grammar.

Instructions:

1. Write a short piece of creative writing, such as a story, poem or essay.

2. Take a break from your work and come back to it, let's say, after 15 minutes. Clear the head. Go outside.

3. Set a time for 10 minutes. During this time, you should revise your work using the following strategies:
   a. Read your work aloud to yourself.
   b. Look for common errors in grammar and spelling.
   c. Check for clarity and flow.
   d. Make any necessary revisions.

4. After the 10 minutes are up, share your revised work with a partner. Partners should provide feedback on the following:
   a. Is the writing clear and easy to understand?
   b. Are the ideas well-organised?
   c. Are there any spelling or grammar errors?
   d. Is the writing engaging and interesting?

5. Students should use the feedback they receive from their partners to make further revisions to their work.

Extension: A checklist for dancing

Create a checklist that you can use to help you revise your work in the future. Your checklist could include items such as:

1. Check for clarity and flow.
2. Make sure the writing is well-organised.
3. Correct any grammar and spelling issues.
4. Ask a trusted friend or family member to read the writing and provide feedback.

CHAPTER 10

Avoiding common mistakes

Last, but certainly not least, is how to avoid common mistakes. Even the most experienced writers can fall into the trap of making silly little errors in the haste to get their writing completed. Believe me, I know. I went over this book a million times before submitting it for editing. I'm sure they found a whole heap of little things. These little things might be grammar and punctuation, spelling or even style and voice. Here are a few common mistakes that I've seen crop up again and again while marking high school work:

- **Subject-verb agreement:** Subjects and verbs must agree in number. A singular subject requires a singular verb, while a plural subject needs a plural verb. For example, 'The cat is playing' is correct, but 'The cats are playing' is also correct.

- **Incorrect tense usage:** Ensure you maintain a consistent tense throughout your writing, unless a shift in time is required. For example, if you start your essay in the past tense, you should continue using the past tense throughout.

- **Run-on sentences:** These occur when two independent clauses are joined without proper punctuation or conjunction. A run-on sentence can be corrected by breaking it into two separate sentences, or by using a conjunction, semicolon or em dash to join the two clauses. For example, the sentence 'I went to the store I bought some groceries' is a run-on sentence. It can be corrected by breaking it into two sentences: 'I went to the store. I bought some groceries.' It can also be corrected by using a conjunction: 'I went to the store and I bought some groceries.'

- **Misplaced or dangling modifiers:** A modifier should be placed next to the word it describes. Otherwise, it can create confusion or unintended meanings. For example, the sentence 'Hopping briskly, the man saw the rabbit with one white ear' confuses the reader as it's not certain who's hopping – the man or the rabbit. A clearer sentence might be: 'The man saw the rabbit with one white ear hopping briskly.'

- **Incorrect punctuation usage:** From comma splices to misused semicolons, punctuation errors can disrupt the flow and clarity of your writing. It's important to know the correct punctuation rules and to use them consistently.

To avoid these mistakes, make it a habit to review grammar rules regularly and proofread your work carefully. You can also use a grammar checker to help you identify errors.

In addition to grammar and punctuation mistakes, high school students should also be aware of other common writing mistakes, such as:

- **Spelling errors and typos:** Spelling mistakes and typos can undermine the credibility of your work. They can distract the reader and make your work seem less professional. To avoid these mistakes, use a spellchecker and proofread your work carefully.

- **Style and voice inconsistencies:** Inconsistencies in style and voice can confuse your readers and dilute your message. It's important to maintain a consistent style and voice throughout your writing. This means using the same tone, level of formality and vocabulary throughout your work.

- **Mixed metaphors:** Mixed metaphors are confusing and should be avoided. A metaphor is a figure of speech that compares two things that are not alike. When you mix metaphors, you compare two things that are even less alike. This can be confusing for the reader.

- **Wordiness:** Wordiness is a common writing problem that can make your writing difficult to read and understand. To avoid wordiness, be concise and avoid using unnecessary words or phrases.

- **Jargon:** Jargon is technical language that is used in a particular field or profession. It can be confusing for readers who are not familiar with the jargon. If you must use jargon, be sure to define it for your readers.

- **Clichés:** Clichés are overused phrases that have lost their meaning. They can make your writing sound boring and unoriginal. Avoid using clichés in your writing.

- **Overreliance on passive voice:** Passive voice is a writing style that puts the subject of the sentence after the verb. It can make your writing sound weak and indirect. Instead of using passive voice, use active voice whenever possible.

Avoiding these kinds of mistakes take practice and attention. Don't be discouraged if you still make errors – the key is to learn from them and keep refining your skills. Finally, remember, every great writer was a beginner once. Jane Austen, Charles Dickens, Steven King – they didn't sit down at their pen and paper, typewriter or computer and instantly bash out a bestseller. It took time and patience. Revising, and revising again.

CONCLUSION

The Writing Cycle

The Writing Cycle: purpose, exploration, ideas, skills, collaboration, publication

This isn't the first book on writing I've written or contributed to; the other title, *Practical Writing Strategies* with Leon Furze, explores in-depth how writing isn't something that just happens. It's an ongoing process. In that title, we devised the Writing Cycle, which consists of a series of steps, each as important as the other, when beginning a writing project.

Here's what the Writing Cycle looks like:

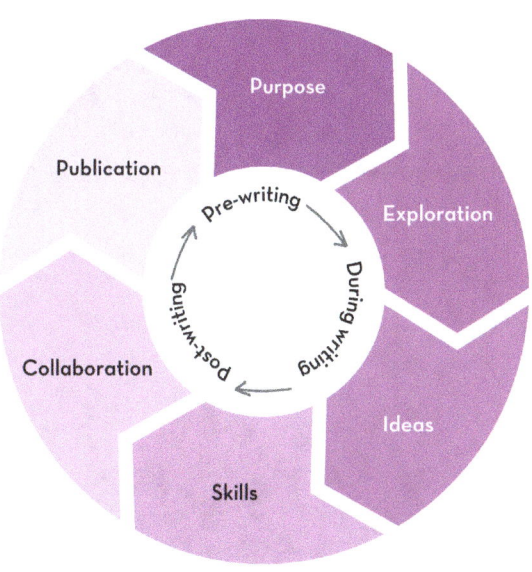

They are briefly outlined below (buy that book if you want them in detail):

- **Purpose:** The reason for writing, the audience, the context and the motivation.
- **Exploration:** Exploring multiple models of quality writing to get a feel for how other authors have approached similar purposes and audiences.
- **Ideas:** Brainstorming, discussions and collaboration. Forming your ideas.
- **Skills:** Identify specific skills to focus on which will support your writing.
- **Collaboration:** Writing isn't a solo exercise. Authors rely on readers, editors and friends. So should you.
- **Publication:** The end of the cycle, or a trigger to go back and start the cycle over. Explore further texts, refine your ideas and skills.

The role of reading in improving writing skills

Reading widely and regularly is one of the most effective ways to improve your writing skills. It exposes you to different writing styles, voices, structures and genres, enriching your understanding of the written word. As you read, you unconsciously absorb grammatical structures, punctuation usage and vocabulary, which can enhance your own writing. Furthermore, reading improves your comprehension skills, critical thinking and creativity – all invaluable tools for a writer.

For example, when you read a novel, you can learn how to develop characters, create a plot and build suspense. When you read a nonfiction book, you can learn about different topics and how to present information concisely. And when you read a newspaper or magazine article, you can see how to write in a concise and persuasive style.

Reading also keeps you informed about various topics, which can provide fodder for your writing. It enables you to see how other writers tackle different themes, develop characters, argue points and engage readers, offering invaluable lessons that you can apply to your own work.

Encouragement to continue writing and improving

Writing, like any other skill, improves with practice. It's crucial to remember that every writer, regardless of their current skill level, started from the beginning. The eloquent essays, engaging stories and compelling articles you admire were crafted through persistent practice, numerous revisions and, often, the courage to face critique and rejection.

So, continue to write, whether it's for assignments, personal expression or professional communication. Embrace the challenges and setbacks as opportunities for growth. Seek feedback, learn from your mistakes and always strive to improve. Experiment with different styles, voices and genres to discover what resonates with you and your audience.

Remember that writing is a journey, not a destination. It's a lifelong process of learning, growing and evolving. Even the most accomplished writers continually seek to improve and adapt their craft. So, keep your pen moving, your keyboard clicking and your mind exploring the endless landscapes of language and imagination. In writing, as in life, the true reward is found not merely in the final product, but in the process of creation. Keep writing, keep learning and keep growing.

FINAL WORD

Specific tips for high school students

- Read a variety of different genres of books, such as fiction, nonfiction, poetry and essays.
- Pay attention to the writing style of the authors you read. What do you like about their style? What could they improve?
- Take note of the vocabulary words you encounter. Look up the definitions of any words you don't know.
- Try to emulate the writing styles and vocabulary of the authors you admire.
- Get feedback on your writing from your teachers, classmates and friends.
- Revise and edit your writing carefully.
- Don't be afraid to experiment with different writing styles and genres.
- Keep writing, even when it's challenging. The more you write, the better you'll become.

www.ingramcontent.com/pod-product-compliance
Lightning Source LLC
Chambersburg PA
CBHW070333120526
44590CB00017B/2859